paris
rooms

ROCKPORT

First published in the United States of America by
Rockport Publishers, Inc.
33 Commercial Street
Gloucester, Massachusetts 01930-5089
Telephone: (978) 282-9590
Facsimile: (978) 283-2742

Distributed to the book trade and art trade in the
United States by North Light Books, an imprint of
F & W Publications
1507 Dana Avenue
Cincinnati, Ohio 45207
Telephone: (800) 289-0963

Other distribution by
Rockport Publishers, Inc.
Gloucester, Massachusetts 01930-5089

ISBN 1-56496-499-x

10 9 8 7 6 5 4 3 2 1

Design: Walter Zekanoski
Cover photo by Brian Harrison, interior design by Thierry Virvaire

About the Designer
Thierry Virvaire was born in Algeria, and, since an early age, has
been passionate about design. After obtaining a business degree in
1983 in Marseilles, he moved to Paris and pursued his studies in the
world of fashion. He has worked as a product manager for Rochas
perfumes, and has designed clothes and jewelry for fashion shows,
while at the same time continuing his interior design work.
Virvaire's joint passions for *haute couture* and interior design has led
to an exciting exchange of ideas. Currently, he is working with
Nicolas Papamiltiades renovating an important Parisian hotel. He
recently designed the wedding dress for his best friend, as well as a
collection of dresses for her friends, including the dress displayed
here. The material is a Designer Guild fabric, chosen for its Eastern
influence, rich colors, and bold patterns—all typical of the designer.

Printed in China.

paris
rooms

**Portfolios of 40
Interior Designers**

STEPHEN MUDGE

GLOUCESTER MASSACHUSETTS

ROCKPORT PUBLISHERS

CONTENTS

IT WAS THE GREAT FRENCH WRITER AND ARTIST Jean Cocteau
who said that the definition of fashion is "that which becomes
unfashionable." The furniture designer Eric Schmitt brought
this quotation to my attention and it is this dilemma that is central
to the work of any interior designer—Are designers creating an
eternal work of art like the Sistine Chapel, or is their role the less
exalted one of producing a temporary decoration, lasting only
until their clients get bored and disrespectfully redecorate? When
interviewing the participants for this book, I was struck by
how differently they saw their roles, from simple arranger of
objects to full-blown architectural artists. Enormous caution was
involved in applying a name to their profession. While some

were eager to rehabilitate the word *décorateur,* it was not a happy choice for the more exalted designers or interior architects.

Good taste or *le bon gout* is central to French life. While the English have their class system and the Americans their income brackets, the French judge each other by their taste or lack of it. To say somebody has poor taste is a harsh and damning criticism. Although Michelle Halard wickedly claims in the book that all her friends have bad taste, it is here that interior designers find their public. To provide a sure-footed, tasteful interior is the dream of every aspiring Frenchman. French style tends to be fairly conservative—finding modern avant-garde creators who have achieved renown is not an easy task. The most famous minimalist

in the book is Christian Liaigre, whose pristine, sleek interiors are much admired, while others such as Eric Caspers Ciborowski or the young Laurent Galle are also in the forefront of contemporary creation, alongside the spectacular furniture of Garouste and Bonetti and Eric Schmitt. The others tend to follow one of two strands: those who produce rigorous, historical, château-style decoration with an eye for immaculate detail and flamboyant luxury; or those who follow a more flexible track mixing and matching from various styles, including ethnic influences and frequent use of 1930s and 1940s furniture and objects.

The towering influence on twentieth-century French decoration was Madeleine Castaing, who opened her boutique during the

German occupation in World War II, selling English furniture and an interpretation of *le style anglais,* a look, which despite its appellation, remains quintessentially French. This style proved a starting point for postwar French interiors, and many of today's designers still speak of Madame Castaing with moist eyes; she lived to a great undisclosed age and continued to hand out formidably firm advice to her clients and colleagues until the end. Even today her shop is a treasure trove of desirable objects, classic wallpapers, and fabrics. Of the 1990s' classics, Jacques Grange is still the name that was most often cited when I was doing research for the book, with the theatrical Jacques Garcia close behind and Graf, the *enfant terrible,* the source of much excited whispering.

My approach to *Paris Rooms* was simple and uncluttered by preconceptions about decoration. I aimed to discover the personalities that make up the rich tapestry of the Parisian design set, passing from one decorator to another rather in the manner of surfing the Internet. "Who else do you think I should see?" was often my parting question and, starting with the superstars, this was how I proceeded. Personal vanity is not an unknown quality in the profession; I was frequently asked who else was in the book and a fair number of eyes were cast skywards! The degree of collaboration also varied from the enthusiastic to the reticent. Unlike in the United States, the concept of selling oneself is not high on the list of priorities of celebrated French

decorators; discretion and aloofness are treasured attributes. Consequently, I am particularly grateful to Alexandre Biaggi, whose magnificent boutique of twentieth-century treasures on the rue de Seine provided many a useful introduction; and to the photographers Roland Beaufre and Guillaume de Laubier, whose suggestions and help were equally invaluable.

Christian
BADIN

ONE OF CHRISTIAN BADIN'S great-grandfathers was the manager of the mighty Gobelins tapestry factory, while the other was a designer and manager of the Sèvres porcelain company. His grandfather pursued a similar career, and his father was himself an interior designer. Small wonder that Badin has one of the most successful careers in French twentieth-century design. His numerous fabric designs, carpets, and furniture have brought him a list of clients that would be the envy of many: Mrs. Kennedy Onassis, Mrs. Paul Mellon, the fashion house Givenchy, the Shah of Iran, and Sheik Yamani. Badin has also designed major exhibitions such as the Watteau tercentenary show at the Grand Palais, Paris. Classical yet contemporary, his interiors represent the best of cool French sophistication, while his garden designs and furniture show a passion for the outdoors rarer in France than in neighboring England.

White curtains edged in black provide an elegant corner beside a picture laden console.

A Louis XVI *secretaire* is set against buttercup yellow walls and flanked by two chairs of the same period.

A mirrored perspective is created above the wide-striped sofa with a Louis XVI bench used as a coffee table.

The library is a light and airy room with a striking rug, Louix XV paneling, and Empire style white armchairs.

Leading from the library, a color-coordinated sofa and wall covering are home to an intriguing porthole.

The view from the bathroom porthole out into the corridor and the countryside beyond.

A luxurious bathroom is found on the other side of the porthole.

CLAUDIO BRIGANTI, AS HIS NAME SUGGESTS, is an Italian from Milan. As a young man he worked as assistant to the great Italian decorator, Mongiardino. His love of Paris led him to set up independently in the capital, where he has a fine reputation for bringing a touch of Southern exuberance to Parisian chic. Briganti himself lays great emphasis on the importance of the work of traditional artisans to his creations. He revels in elaborate painted fabrics and stenciled wall effects. For these he prizes the work of a dedicated and increasingly rare breed of specialist collaborators—be it the extraordinary painter on fabric, Denise Olivier, who can create anything from a complex, painted floor covering to a simple design on a curtain; or Sophia Zorka for her subtle dying processes, whereby a sheet of velvet can be magically transformed into an aged, sun-faded fabric of romantic origin. Briganti's innate Italian elegance guarantees his international clientele an original hand-crafted decoration.

The long parquet floored billiard room has landscape scenes delicately painted on the panels in the ceiling, in contrast to the straight unadorned silk curtains.

The hallway abounds in Briganti's painted effects, both on the trompe l'oeil paneling and the vaulted ceiling. The atmosphere is resolutely neo-Gothic.

The salon is given a typical Briganti touch with the alternating wall covering of blue damask and cottonade panels, including the curtains. The room's centerpiece is the beautiful Aubusson carpet, crowned by a nineteenth-century chandelier.

Here Briganti found a particularly beautiful Chinese wallpaper to adorn this elegantly alcoved bathroom.

The copper bath mounted on a wooden plinth is framed by what appears to be two cupboards. In fact, behind the painted mirrored doors there is a shower on one side and a WC on the other. A crystal chandelier adds to the fantasy.

The bedroom shows Briganti in a playfully creative mood. The embossed pattern on the walls, echoed on the blind, makes for an eye-catching backdrop to the bamboo bed and kilim-style carpet.

IN ONE OF THE PRETTIEST SQUARES on the Left Bank, previously home to the artist Eugène Delacroix, is the Manuel Canovas boutique, which together with the firm Nobilis is the capital's leading supplier of wallpaper and matching fabrics. Although the designer's empire was taken over a couple years ago, the boutique and the Canovas name go from strength to strength, the inimitable decorative style still bearing the touch of the master. Son of the artist and fabric designer Blas Canovas de Lorca, Manuel Canovas pursued his career via the Beaux Arts in Paris and the Villa Medicis in Rome, founding his first company in 1963. By the mid-1970s he was directing a highly successful multinational business, his name becoming synonymous with quality wall coverings and fabrics. Interestingly, Canovas also studied archaeology in Mexico and is an enthusiastic collector of sand and rocks from his travels. This parallel passion has influenced the designer's style and use of color, as is reflected in his own home featured here.

A diamond patterned carpet is used in the paneled library, which features a sweeping staircase leading to a mezzanine, allowing ease of access to the collection, as well as being a striking architectural feature.

The bedroom is a medley of minty pastel colors with a striking multicolored, diamond-motif carpet. These colors are taken up by the fabric on the bed and its drapery. The Canovas wallpaper of pale green foliage completes the soft informal atmosphere. The transparent shelved tables contain the designer's shell collection, which together with the rock-style side console reflect Canovas's archaeological background.

The Canovas carpet with its simple intercepting diamonds on a beige background is set off by the rich yellow curtains. The classical French stone mantelpiece is home to an Indian statue flanked by two glass-domed candles and a simple oriental flower. A model Asian pagoda stands to one side, while the large wrought-iron and glass table by Giacometti is noticeable for some interesting wildlife around the base.

CHINESE EXPORT PORCELAIN
IN NORTH AMERICA

THE AGE OF
CORREGGIO
AND THE
CARRACCI

National Gallery of Art, Washington
The Metropolitan Museum of Art, New York
Pinacoteca Nazionale, Bologna

ESSIONISM AND
IMPRESSIONISM

IF THERE IS ONE NAME that epitomizes Parisian chic, it is that of Madeleine Castaing. Her Left Bank gallery on the rue Jacob remains an Aladdin's cave for any potential interior designer. She opened her first shop selling English furniture during the German occupation, a daringly audacious idea. Her success was such that it is impossible to discuss twentieth-century French interiors without reference to her work. All of Paris has passed through her doors, and she was a personality of such intensity that even in her nineties she retained a sparkle in her eye which demanded respect. After her death her country home was sold to the cineast James Ivory, but her gallery continues to supply objects with that unmistakable Castaing touch. According to Castaing, "Making your home is a creative act. I create homes like other people write poetry, compose music, or paint, and my home captures a better likeness than a portrait. Don't draw back from bold ideas, but boldness informed by taste (a quality, an infinitely rarer gift than we think, both personal and creative). As well as this you need intuition, vigor; deciding what to lose is difficult, everything is modified according to personality, place, and climate."

A delightful painted passageway of faded Gallic shades, romantic fabric-hung paneling and a classic Castaing carpet.

An intimate corner of a Parisian apartment abounding in Castaing fabrics, gently lit by a porcelain lamp.

An original, untouched Castaing design for a Parisian client, where the mainly eighteenth-century English furniture was chosen by Castaing herself. The now classic Castaing matching carpets and fabrics are complemented by her preferred conical shaped sidelamps, creating a Parisian look that remains the epitome of *le bon gout*.

Castaing's very feminine bedroom features her own pink-striped paper that adds a dusty atmosphere to the whole room, which is dominated by the impressive iron and brass bedstead. The room is lit by a collection of typical Castaing sidelamps with pink shades. Below the gilded mirror over the mantel is a comforting nineteenth-century chaise longue.

Another corner of Castaing's bedroom, showing her dressing table littered with photos of *le tout Paris*. Here the Louis XV gilded furniture benefits from the soft elegance of the designer.

Castaing interior set up for an informal party.

A rare glimpse into the intimate world of Madeleine Castaing; her own apartment has been preserved just as she left it. In the salon we find a good example of her classic blue fabric and matching carpet, where her collection of mainly eighteenth-century English furniture is casually placed, lit by a suspended brass lamp with her trademark conical lampshades.

A nod to Castaing's English taste with a table laid for afternoon tea with English bone china. The room is lit by an original Murano crystal chandelier, which casts a gentle light onto the eighteenth-century china display cabinet.

François Catroux was born in Algeria and moved to France when he was fourteen. A designer since 1967, Catroux opened his own firm in 1968, which now employs six people under his personal direction and is highly respected in the capital for its Right Bank good taste. When asked to describe his interiors Catroux says, "My designs are simple, always emphasizing the architecture, the volume, and the distribution of space." Among Catroux's diverse influences and interests are a love of English charm and comfort, as well as a clear eye for the consistency and strength of elements within a given place. His international projects, which number about a dozen per year, include residences in Paris, New York, London, Geneva, Gstaad, Saint Moritz, Greece, Saudi Arabia, Jordan, and Japan. Catroux's interest does not lie in the size of the project, but in its quality or originality. Recently he has completed several designs for Henri Bendel in the United States.

François Catroux's salon is an exciting mix of contemporary design and thirties and forties chic. The round table was designed by Catroux and the day bed is a signed Mies van der Rohe. The striking pair of table lamps are from the 1930s, while the mahogany armchair in the foreground is contemporary, looking well on the braided needlepoint rug by Etamine.

In the library, the stained oak bookcases are complemented by a sofa and table designed by Catroux and a forties armchair by Jansen. The eye-catching contemporary picture is by Gondoin.

Another view of the salon, showing Catroux's skillful use of African art, combined with forties sculpture and his own furniture. On the Catroux-designed table there is a sculpture by Van Stuck and on either side of the chimney are colonial statues, each holding globes. On the right is a magnificent African mask from the Upper Volta, and in the alcoves are two pastels by Lambert-Rucki.

The kitchen is entirely in oak, dominated by the overhead wine rack. The table is by Alinéa from Avignon standing under the designer's collection of twentieth-century art.

The bedroom is warmly decorated with a fabric wall covering by Casal and a striped textile by Athena, which is placed chessboard fashion behind the bed. The standard lamp on the left is by Laurence Montado and the cashmere bedspread by Yves St. Laurent.

AFTER STUDIES AT THE Arts Appliqués and Beaux Arts in Paris, Eric Caspers Ciborowski became fascinated by the pictorial style of the early twentieth century, in particular the style of the symbolists, surrealists, and the Bauhaus. His research, based on solid architectural principles, extended to the environment and lifestyles. His early experience, working with two established decorators on a new town in southwest France, defined his decorative ambitions. His work is based on the personality and psychological makeup of his clients, including prominent collectors, creating a vital link with this and his own aesthetic and cultural considerations. Ciborowski is not content simply to create beautiful interiors and gardens but makes a conscious effort to create a style devolved from history and specific artistic movements. His designs are the fruit of great research into colors and the choice of suitable objects, but also the desire to explore the spatial principles of architecture. Currently he is working on a house in Marrakesh for an American client, an ancient factory in Brittany built by Vauban, and is looking forward to a project to decorate a yacht.

Ciborowski's flame-shaped side lights illuminate the strong architectural features, which are emphasized by the sharply contrasting color scheme.

Another view of the same space. The Le Corbusier armchairs and striking use of a brilliant red carpet and column give the whole room an expressionist and Bauhaus atmosphere.

Here the architectural details of the grill at the windows give the room more of an Art Nouveau feel, while the saffron and gold colors provide a warmer cosseting aspect.

The loosely hung, heavy brown curtains at a stained-glass window in front of a plain white sofa give this corner a gothic revival look, emphasized by the standing chalice.

An Islamic shaped bookcase sets the tone for this room. The colors of the oriental-style center lantern are picked up in the constructionalist painting.

Another view of the same room showing a 1940s cupboard by Prouvé.

A grand neoclassical mood is set by the Egyptian style sphinx and early twentieth-century bust. The draped curtains and irregular stagey structures give the whole room a theatrical touch.

AGNES COMAR OPENED HER FIRST SHOP on the rue de Seine, Paris, and quickly became internationally renowned for her best-selling cushions. In 1980, she moved to her current premises, 7 avenue Georges V, a prestigious address where she welcomes an international clientele. In addition to her collections of fabrics, Agnes Comar is equally at home as an interior designer, numbering the Cartier boutiques, Champagne Mumm's guest house, and numerous villas and apartments for private clients amongst her commissions. Refinement, delicacy, subtlety, and harmony are the hallmarks of her intimate style. She believes that decoration should be flexible, dependent on the play of details, dynamic yet serene, breathing life into the building. For this to happen, objects must be able to be moved, spaces to transform themselves, and the occupant to add his or her own personal touches. Agnes Comar knows that her own creations stand up well to diverse marriages of style and period. Comar is the epitome of a Parisienne: rigorous yet imaginative, intellectual yet sensitive. Her very feminine style, led by her rich and inventive fabrics, hides an acute professional, whose clients value her practical genius to create traditional splendor with a contemporary talent.

The exotic fruit and vegetables provide the theme for this tented Kasbah style bedroom. Comar's natural brown and white counterpane on a low safari bed is complemented by the Moroccan standard lamp and a fabric suspended gilded oval frame.

Drapery of one of Comar's fabrics achieves a dramatic effect, making the curtains a real feature of the decoration.

A fine wooden four-poster bed on neutral coconut matting is transformed into a comfortable daybed by a pair of swagged cushions at either end and a tonal mix of creams and browns creating a real cascade of Comar cushions.

Robert
D'ARIO

"A HOUSE IS LIKE A MEETING; we are, in time, only temporary passengers within its walls; love your house and it will return your love…" says Robert d'Ario, who loves his houses with unbounded generosity. His own country home is an eighteenth-century Palladian villa, a former residence of the president of the ancient parliament of Aix en Provence, decorated with meticulous care. Of country life he says, "One must have a love of friendship; country houses, where time stands still, allow you to live a happy complicity of shared feelings and to transform a dream into reality." Like the writer La Fontaine, he enjoys flowers, fruit, and music, avoiding stiff solemnity in his decoration with imaginative personal touches. He prefers antique furniture and makes abundant use of precious silks and chintz, often recreating original antique patterns. d'Ario is considered a decorator of rare sophistication, with just a touch of extravagance.

There is a loving, luxurious atmosphere in this blue salon. Notice the arranged "disorder" on the coffee table. The Regency chairs covered in leopard skin and the late eighteenth-century Indian buffalo horn lend the whole room a touch of fantasy and exoticism.

The bathroom, flooded with light, shows the designer's joyous hedonism. A Languedoc marble bath crowns the room, decorated with views of Venice reflecting the designer's Italian heritage.

A play of garnet reds leads you from the library to the bedroom, where you can glimpse the bed covered by a Chinese fur counterpane.

A gilded bamboo desk and rich colors and fabrics adorn this intimate corner.

The dining room is bathed in a soft light by the coarse silk, straw-colored double curtains. The walls are decorated with painted Chinese scenes, very fashionable in the eighteenth century. The mahogany table is laid with fine porcelain and Charles X cut glasses.

The fairy tale bedroom is decorated with recreated antique fabrics in gray and blue and one of the designer's favorite elaborately draped Tester beds.

JUST BESIDE THE LOUVRE on the Quai Voltaire (and a few doors down from the late Rudolf Nureyev's apartment) is the Galerie Camoin, center of the activities of one of the great figures of French interior design, Alain Demachy. Since 1980 he has divided his time between his work as decorator and that of his antique gallery, but the Galerie Camoin is no ordinary antique emporium. High-ceilinged rooms overlooking the Seine succeed one another, each decorated with the furniture and accessories from a different period, a sumptuous museum and design center combined. Demachy himself studied at the Ecole Speciale d'Architecture and went on to collaborate with celebrated international architects on projects ranging from grand hotels and restaurants to palaces and apartments for the rich and famous, including crowned heads of Europe, the private residences of the Rothchilds, and an apartment for Johnny Halliday, France's most famous rocker, and his wife Sylvie Vartan. Demachy also designs his own limited edition furniture and accessories, his name providing proof of unequaled quality and craftsmanship.

A life-size basketball sculpture dominates this stylish salon. This decoration designed by Demachy over 20 years ago now looks as completely contemporary as it did at the time. The eighteenth-century Chinese ancestral portrait is placed over an Italian lamp by Aulenti. The carpet is designed by Demachy.

This house was designed by Demachy for clients in the Bahamas and features treated pine screens, the color achieved by a process called "pickling." At the end of the room is a mosaic made up entirely of seashells. The neo-Egyptian coffee table is in bronze, in keeping with the light colonial style of the room.

The airy bedroom with its louvered shutters has a stronger Chinese accent given by the rug and wicker garden stool used as an occasional table.

VOTED CREATEUR DE L'ANNÉE in 1998 by *Maison et Objet,* Olivier Gagnère's career has gained strength over the past ten years. He is very much a designer rather than a decorator, but the interiors that he invests with his very individual objects and accessories take on a distinctive Gagnère look. His work has been frequently exhibited in the Galerie Maeght, Paris, and the Galerie Néotù in Paris and New York, where his collections of porcelain, lamps, and furniture have taken on classic status; examples of his work are found in the Musée des Arts Décoratifs and the Musée National Georges Pompidou, Paris, as well as the Museum of Modern Art, San Francisco. Gagnère's name came to the fore for his stunning contribution to the Café Marly, realized in collaboration with Yves Taralon. He has enjoyed a long and productive relationship with the china company Bernardau, creating several of their lines as well as the decoration of their store in New York and their salon de thé in the rue Royale, Paris. This year he has just completed a commission for a new Pastis glass for Ricard, a clear stamp of national approval.

A close-up of a milk jug and plate by Gagnère, showing the influence of Picasso.

Theatrical golden chairs provide the setting for a collection of Gagnère's porcelain.

A chic corner of the Louvre's fashionable Café Marly. Gagnère's furnishing contributes to a very special atmosphere, which successfully provides a postmodern aesthetic without betraying the splendor of the original building.

The designer's bedroom has an ethnic counterpane and wall hanging, which provide a backdrop for a collection of oval oil paintings. The atmosphere is completed by a nineteenth-century birdcage.

The bright ethnic throw over the canape, the leopard design on the occasional chair and the colorful rugs are in sharp contrast with the dark formal walls and the simple console covered with the designer's collection of books and paintings.

"TO SHARE YOUR IDEAS, to prove the validity of those ideas, and then to realize them with success brings the greatest pleasure"— this is how the young designer Laurent Galle, tipped for great success in the twenty-first century, sums up his approach to interior design. Galle works for a growing private and commercial clientele, who appreciate his fiery creative passion combined with an attention to detail to achieve an end result that is both imaginative yet practical and harmonious. His style is resolutely contemporary but with an unusually deep respect for the tastes and needs of his clients. He lays great emphasis on the importance of discussing and clarifying his ideas with his clients to find the *ton juste* for each commission. As he says, "One must continually adapt one's ideas according to the building and the people who live in it, respecting their opinions and taste without losing the 'soul' of the project. Dialogue is essential; an intimate exchange is then established which becomes enriching for both parties. Nothing can be created without this balance."

The high-tech kitchen with its integrated spotlights and floor design focuses attention firmly on the table.

A free-standing staircase rises up to dramatic effect between two twentieth-century pictures. The tiger stripe carpet is also by Galle.

The peach flushed salon features Galle's spectacular canape and carpet. Beside the draped silk curtains are two engraved glass panels.

Two urns announce the entrance to the bay window, where a nineteenth-century chaise lounge stands on Galle's swirling carpets looking out through the elaborately draped silk curtains.

Another corner of the salon with a Galle canape and carpet. Notice the imaginative way in which the radiator is hidden by a floating cloud.

In 1992, JACQUES GARCIA became the owner of an eighteenth-century château and has set about restoring both buildings and gardens to their former glory, an apt task for one of the undoubted aristocrats of Parisian decorators. The many prestigious projects with which his name is associated include the 6000-square-meter apartment of the Sultan of Brunei on the Place Vendôme, a replica of the chateau de Champs sur Marne for a collector in Houston, Texas, and the interior design concept of the Meridien and Sofitel hotels. His international clients appreciate his refined and faultless good taste. Today he explains his work thus: "My real love and understanding of objets d'art have led me to accept the framework corresponding to a specific period, recreating the spirit of the past, while retaining the principal objective to produce a living atmosphere, far from any museum-like concept."

Anyone for snooker? The game room of the château features magnificent eighteenth-century paneling, French gilded furniture and light fittings of the same period.

A full-length view of the long gallery. Here one can see how the plaster Egyptian statues punctuate the gallery. In the foreground is a beautiful embossed carpet and eye-catching, pale green silk blinds that match the rich green walls. The animal skin thrown over the sofa and the plethora of objects, oil lamps and candles contribute to a "grand tour" style of decoration, very much a Garcia specialty.

The marbled grand hall is sparely impressive, lined with Greco-Roman statuary. Garcia's hand is apparent in the subtle gilding of the doors and painting of the baroque ceiling.

The tapestry-lined bedroom, lit by a Murano crystal chandelier, has an impressive seventeenth-century canopied bed on a blue Persian silk carpet, beside an elaborate brocaded bench.

Another angle of the bedroom shows the splendid eighteenth-century Cartel clock dominating the mirrored mantelpiece, over an amusing model canon. Here you can appreciate the fine detail of the paneling and the romantic reflection of the tapestry opposite.

One end of the château's long gallery with a stuffed parrot in the foreground. Garcia's sense of opulence is striking; from the gilded bookcases to the decorative Egyptian statues that line the gallery, the daring theatricality is excitingly "over the top."

"THE OLDEST PROFESSION IN THE WORLD" is how Henri Garelli mischievously describes his work as an interior architect. This is a typically outspoken comment from this charming man, something of a late twentieth-century dandy, which hides a deep passion and respect for the profession he has exercised for over twenty-five years. As a young man in Saint Tropez (where he still has a gallery selling pictures, antiques, and his own furniture), Garelli traveled widely, as influenced by English comfort as by Italian sensuality.

He works mostly on projects for a loyal private clientele, including the country home of his friend, the artist Bernard Buffet. The cream cool chic of the apartment he designed for Parisian clients is only one aspect of his work; he also has an abiding passion for neoclassical, but here he decided to create 1940s decor, both light and ephemeral. He enjoyed the notion that everything should be easy to dismantle and transplant elsewhere. "My clients," says Garelli, "are thoroughly civilized people, but it's still a heavy challenge to invent a living space for people who blow in and out of town like the wind." Henri Garelli is himself a highly civilized epicurean man, working to the sound of classical music, always aware of the need to combine comfort with aestheticism. He creates interiors for the pleasure of others with an unusual seriousness of purpose: "The profession is one of thinker and producer, a great artistic profession, which inhabits one's whole being. We should rehabilitate this work, which is not a profession for snobs or imbeciles...."

The dining room is the most elaborate room in the apartment, with walls covered in painted canvas. The studded gilded chairs are nineteenth-century English, while the 1940s table is in marble and gilded bronze. The room is dominated by the imposing pair of candelabras by Polillerat.

In a corner of the bedroom, a 1940s parchment desk and a 1910 armchair stand next to a studded raffia screen by Garelli. The green and white striped curtains are made of Florentine cotton, also used to cover the sofa in the study.

Garelli's Cagolin rug, the Giacometti light fitting, and the pleated wall covering are all echoed in the main salon.

The salon features two sofas covered in an African style by Le Manach. The sofas as well as the Cagolin rug were designed by Garelli. The walls are covered in pleated wall hangings, creating a column-like effect. The room is lit by a 1940s Giacometti light for Jean-Michael Frank.

"LES NOUVEAUX BARBARES" was how the press dubbed the design team of Garouste and Bonetti when they made their design debut in 1981 with the "Barbare" collection for the Jansen house of interior design in Paris. Their partnership had begun just a year earlier when Paris-trained set designer Elizabeth Garouste and her husband, the painter Gerard Garouste, were commissioned to design the "Privilège" nightclub in Paris and invited Lugano-born textile designer and stylist Mattia Bonetti to join them. The professional relationship blossomed and the result is a design partnership of worldwide renown. Their furniture and objects have been featured in exhibitions at the Pompidou Center, Paris, the Victoria and Albert Museum, London, and numerous individual exhibitions in Japan, Germany, and the United States. Since 1991 they have devoted more of their time to residences. As well as their erudite and sophisticated furniture, their work extends from the designing of the "Hommage to Max Ernst" footbridge in Quimper to the flacon designs for Nina Ricci perfumes.

The entrance hall to this apartment in Hong Kong, which Garouste and Bonetti designed for private clients, is typical of their fine work in wrought iron, casting a patterned shadow onto the marble floor.

A marbled area is home to a Francis Bacon and a sculpture by Henry Moore, the whole area announced by a spectacular Garouste and Bonetti tripod standard lamp.

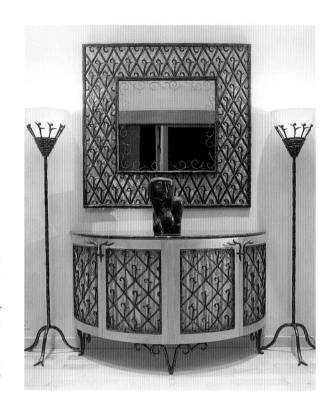

Garouste and Bonetti's style is immediately recognizable in this wrought iron and wood console, surrounded by matching wrought iron standard lamps and mirror.

A gaming area features a ceramic dish by the designers, the floating lines of which are taken up by the curving metal lines of Garouste and Bonetti's pair of cupboards.

Elizabeth Garouste's own salon features wall hangings and a sculpture by her husband Gerard, the stripped wood over the mantel giving a hint of the Garouste and Bonetti look.

THE NEXT TIME you are in the Metropolitan Museum Shop in New York take another look—the shop was designed by one of France's most talented young interior architects, Eric Gizard. His Left Bank company has been in business for the last ten years and has completed such important commissions as the Tourist Office for the Ile de France, and shops for Habitat and Daum crystal, both in Paris and New York. He tends to design private apartments for his friends; as he says, "It's easier to conceive a space for someone you know." His style combines a certain classicism with the use of traditional materials, often with an ethnic feel, while his practical commercial experience ensures that any Gizard apartment will be not only stylish but also easy to live in. He enjoys collecting objects and bric-à-brac from the flea markets of Paris, all of which he can incorporate into harmonious decoration. When asked what guides the choices in his own apartment he replies, "My own taste and intuition." Regarding his use of color he says, "All the colors blend with each other; it's just a question of proportions and balance."

Gizard's corded podium bed is framed by tented Moroccan fabric and lit by a paper lamp by Noguchi. A ballet bar is used as an ingenious clothes hanger.

The mint green hallway of the designer's flat sets the eclectic tone typical of Gizard's work. Everything is found here from a Louis XVI chair to a sideboard left in its original distressed condition.

Under a spectacular black and white photograph by Bianca Sforni, the salon features two armchairs by Réné Gabriel opposite two Habitat maxi cushions on a Moroccan carpet. The table is in sycamore supported by Knoll bases found in the local flea market.

Under a metal Moroccan wall lamp, a table covered in a Pakistani material is home to a riot of objects and ethnic holiday souvenirs.

DIDIER GOMEZ BEGAN HIS CAREER in 1978 by creating the immediately successful First Time, an interior design consultancy with associated furniture stores. In 1985 he opened his own firm, employing fifteen people, allowing him to have overall control of major projects right down to the smallest detail. His meticulously designed contemporary furniture, lights, fabrics, and floor coverings have led to commissions from leading companies throughout the world, including: Yves Saint-Laurent, Jean Paul Gaultier, Rodier, Cartier, and Rolex. His list of high-flying private clients is no less impressive, with the homes of Pierre Bergé, Daniel Auteuil, and Harrison Ford to his credit. This success story has led Gomez to be responsible for some spectacular Parisian inner city projects, notably the Carousel du Louvre, the new shopping complex under the Louvre, for which he was the artistic director, and the director's office and conference room of the new Bastille Opera. Since 1994 Gomez has formed a partnership with the architect Jean Jacques Ory, forming the company Ory Gomez, with a subsidiary company in Hong Kong, O.G. Design Ltd.

The director's office at the Bastille Opera has a relaxed informal atmosphere. Gomez delights in the use of contrasting woods, from the African sculpture to the wooden paneling via his own semi-circular desk and lattice covered chairs.

There is an oriental rigor about Gomez's decoration of the Opera Bastille conference room, dominated by the long surfboard-style wooden table. The attention to detail is remarkable, from the high-tech lights to the stylish paint effects.

In Didier Gomez's own apartment, the use of classical columns lends this practical library and music area a certain grandeur in contrast to the simply blinded window.

François-Joseph
GRAF

"FRANÇOIS-JOSEPH GRAF is probably the only décorateur today who knows how to meld rigor with fantasy." This is how Pierre Berge, the Yves St. Laurent fashion magnet, describes Paris's most glittering *enfant terrible* of late twentieth-century interior architecture. Indeed, the concept of architecture is paramount in Graf's philosophy: "Decoration, anyone can do it. What is important is to construct the appropriate architectural proportions. That is the real *métier,* and to do it one needs great knowledge of art history and respect for the past." Graf attained this respect for the past not only from his training, but also during three years as assistant to the curator at the chateau of Versailles. "Versailles gives you a feeling for proportions. You go from gigantic rooms with ceilings ten meters high to minuscule ones two meters high. It teaches one the sense of harmony to be achieved in a house, the rhythm between grand and small rooms, between light and shadow. It is the most beautiful school in the world." It is a schooling that has earned the designer an enviable reputation, be it for his apartments, the tapestried elegance of Paris's top restaurant, L'Ambroisie, or magnificent hotels such as La Mirande in Avignon. His rigorous style does not preclude a strong personal relationship with his clients; "a project evolves and a decorator does his work *with* the client, not *for,* but *with.*"

A blazing fire and candlelit table highlight the warm colors of the carpet and pale green double doors.

A Chinese silk wall hanging and a collection of blue and white porcelain give this corner of the salon a chinoiserie feel. The rich choice of fabrics creates a warm cosseting atmosphere typical of Graf.

An intimate corner of a bedroom, where a fabric-covered screen provides discreet protection for the writing desk; the whole area decorated in soft floral textiles.

The bathroom retains the comfortable country style with its French grey paneled doors and warm orange curtains.

This bedroom is one of traditional comfort, the mood taken from the architectural details above the doors. The brass bed is set against an especially designed floral wallpaper.

JACQUES GRANGE, CHEVALIER DES ARTS ET DES LETTRES, is without doubt considered by many as the doyen of French decorators. After working briefly with the great Henri Samuel and later Alain Demachy, he began working independently in 1970 and the rest is, as they say, history. His classical French good taste is often imitated but seldom equaled, and it is this consistency that has earned Grange a veritable who's who of celebrity clients. Be it Paris's leading restaurants, Alain Ducas or Ledoyen, Princess Caroline's yacht and home in Monaco, Yves Saint Laurent's boutiques and private homes in Paris and Marrakesh, all have been blessed by a Grange decoration. If you are shopping at Paloma Picasso's in New York or Dior in Honolulu, then the same man is behind the design. Even when designing for museums, Grange plays for the highest stakes, having been invited by the Louvre to decorate the Musée des Arts de la Mode. Despite his busy schedule, Gange finds time to pursue his passion for collecting nineteenth- and twentieth-century objects and paintings.

A double height artist's studio with Saint Sulpice just visible in the distance. A Comagnie des Indes style chair and a marble bust on an artist's plinth give a bohemian yet refined atmosphere with a basket of logs ready for the fireplace.

A plunging view of the same studio from the staircase. Notice the elegant contrast between the light wood and the sea-green carpet. Over the sofa hangs a spectacular tapestry of Don Giovanni and the commendatore, making full use of the room's height, whilst above the fireplace is a theatrical stone relief. In the corner is another element essential to an artist's studio, a folding screen. A Murano crystal chandelier complements the natural light.

The carved North African–style table gives a Moorish feel to this saffron-colored corner. The wooden screen effectively frames the wall-hanging behind.

Symmetrically placed folding tables between two windows with elaborately draped double curtains are home to a collection of antique masks. The red of the high-backed buttoned chair is gently reflected by tulips sitting on a sober wooden console.

This fashionable neo-1940s Parisian study is dominated by an antique
writing desk over which hangs a portrait by Tchelichew.

A directoire-style chandelier crowns this classical marble bathroom with an
elegant period double wash basin console. The cool cream curtains lead
onto a balcony with a view over the roofs of Paris.

ELDEST SON OF THE DESIGN GIANT NOBILIS, Yves Halard opened his first furniture showroom in 1950 on the Right Bank, before expanding to larger prestigious premises in the heart of the Latin Quarter on the fashionable Boulevard St. Germain. His wife, Michelle Halard, is one of the capital's most respected decorators. A fascinating character of firm yet permissive ideas, her decoration with its eclectic mix of styles and periods remains a classic example of French good taste. "In decoration," she says, "you have to abandon all preconceived ideas. To those who don't know what to do, I say 'Be yourself.' Your own spontaneity, even your ignorance, will give better results than any imposed ideas. All my friends have bad taste and that's fine by me." A mischievous comment, but Halard believes that like a person, decoration should be in constant evolution and one should have the courage to dare to be audacious. "I am often surprised to see ladies in the boutique with a sample of material in their hand desperately looking for the precise color that will 'go' with it. Anything will 'go' if it expresses your personality."

The kitchen's powder-blue dresser and units create a country atmosphere. We can appreciate Halard's love of a profusion of objects; here pots, pans and porcelain.

The bathroom is a far cry from clinical technology with its comforting collection of pictures and nineteenth-century fittings, commode, and towel stand in front of a stone chimney piece.

A jumble of books and objects characterize Halard's library, presided over by a Gothic revival chandelier. Within its warm green tones, books are here to be read and not used as a decorative feature.

A saffron yellow corner of Michelle Halard's salon. Notice the typical Halard contrasts of period, a Louis XV "chauffeuse" chair standing beside a modern semi-circular tripod occasional table. The color scheme is also daring, combining the saffron walls with browns and pinks from the colorful kilim.

THERE IS AN ELEMENT OF THE ROMANTIC HERO in the story of Daniel Hamel's early apprenticeship: leaving his native France to practice his chosen profession in the United States, being taken on by the celebrated firm of Jansen, before returning home to become the English representative of the great Henri Samuel. It is training to which few of today's young designers can aspire. Hamel's rigorously structured spatial design pays tribute to his illustrious masters, while his interiors are graced with objects chosen with a highly individual collector's eye. Now based in France, he works for a private international clientele with whom he enjoys long and loyal collaborations.

Hamel's favorite period is Louis XVI for its refined elegance, but he does not believe in strict historical reproductions, favoring the mixing of styles and periods with striking yet always harmonious results. The small apartment featured here shows his judicious use of space, as well as a perfectionist's attention to detail and proportion.

A marvelous effect created by *portières* drapery around the mirrored chimney piece, lending height and reflected light to the apartment. On the marble mantelpiece stands a smooth dark bronze Renaissance sculpture.

A grand late Renaissance portrait hangs over the Louis XVI desk arranged with chinoiserie objects. The atmosphere throughout is one of chiaroscuro, the subtle play of candlelight and natural light on the decoration.

A view looking through the salon into the bedroom. The bookcase was designed by Hamel especially for the apartment; on either side stand Louis XVI *Bergère* chairs. Just visible is the twentieth-century golden coffee table, a daring yet successful combination.

A porthole in the rich green entrance hall gives natural light to the bathroom, the blue delft wall hangings being the only decorative feature.

The bedroom cupboards were designed by Hamel and feature fabric panels that match the diamond patterned wallpaper.

FOLLOWING IN THE FOOTSTEPS of Chateaubriand and Stendhal, Jacques Leguennec's life was changed by a visit to Rome. In the elegant proportions and nuanced ochres of the eternal city he found inspiration for his own furniture designs. With the painter Alain Ozane he formed a partnership which formed the basis of the "Atelier Jacques Leguennec." Leguennec creates the forms and models, while Onzain, the painter, brings the patina. For the construction of his furniture Leguennec uses French artisans with pride: "In France there are so many talented artisans who don't know how to best exploit their possibilities. There are still so many things left to be created in France." Leguennec does not limit his operations to furniture design, but is also an enthusiastic and experienced decorator. He says of his work in this domain, "My furniture is comfortable and goes just as well in a contemporary decoration as it does in a period one. In times of crisis, classicism becomes an increasingly known quantity. Personally I have always been attracted by a rather classical decoration. I am attracted by elegance and refinement and reject complaisance and mediocrity."

Leguennec's light and airy library draws attention to his handmade book-cases with a subtle pale patina.

Surrounded by his bookcases, Leguennec's bedroom is a reader's paradise. The designer's two-tier ebony bedside tables and lamps contrast well with the pale wood of the bookcase.

Behind the protective gaze of a sculpted monkey, we find one of Leguennec's wooden chimney pieces amongst a typically nineteenth-century profusion of pictures.

An elegant corner with Leguennec's ebony chair and lamp stand, set against an off-white silk curtain.

A typical Parisian demi-lune window frames a desk and rich study-green covered chair, which show Leguennec at his most classical.

CHRISTIAN LIAIGRE, WHOSE PRIVATE HOME is featured here, is one of the few Parisian interior architects who have adopted a contemporary approach to design. Liaigre was a student at the Ecole Superieure des Arts Decoratifs in Paris, and formed his own company in 1987, producing not only interior concepts but also furniture especially designed in limited editions for top architects. The showroom of his furniture in Paris is one of the most spectacular of its kind in the city, but you can also see his work in one of the capital's trendiest hotels, the Montalembert, which quickly became the choice of the fashion conscious. His project for the Villa Medicis in Rome shows the breadth of his range and influence. He believes the phenomenal success of his design work is based on attention to detail, only producing items of the highest quality, and the conception of furniture specific to an individual project. Currently he is working on the 7,000 square meters of the famous Selfridges department store in London and the New York apartment of Calvin Klein.

The rich brown wood-surrounded bath is a twentieth-century interpretation of a Victorian classic.

Christian Liaigre's Parisian apartment is designed along pure minimalist lines. Downstairs the white walls and open staircase throw the attention onto Liaigre's ebonized chairs, side table and mouse-grey velvet sofa.

The white paneled walls provide texture and background for Liaigre's off-white easy chairs, while not encroaching on the intentional spareness, whereas the ornate chimney is used as a purely decorative element.

The kitchen's only anecdotal items are the food itself and some antique kitchen implements, but the turned-wood stools around the black trestle table have something of a country feel.

A wicker and straw motif dominates the other bedroom, the low divans sporting especially designed headboards while comfort is provided by Liaigre's corded armchairs.

Contemporary rusticity reduces a four-poster bed to a refined minimum, while the paneled ceiling and polished parquet look back to bygone times.

THE WORD *FEMININE* IN ALL ITS POSITIVE COMPLEXITY could well have been invented to describe the decoration of Sabine Marchal. Her boutique on Paris's elegant rue de Bourgogne, Nuit Blanche, is a sumptuous assortment of household linens and accessories amid blissful domesticity. All are designed or chosen to reflect Marchal's romantic spirit and love of comfort. However, this lady has more than one string to her bow. She has designed an ultra-modern, high-tech studio for her son, where you will look in vain for floral frills, while another branch of her activity is the business Techn'art. This venture offers Marchal's savoir faire to entrepreneurs in the decoration of entrance halls and common parts of buildings, a task to which she brings her quintessential Gallic sense of refinement. She confides, "Be it a private apartment or a big complex, I want to give them all some of my joie de vivre, my enthusiasm, my gaiety." By all accounts she succeeds.

Marchal's collection of blue plates and vases from the Chinese market, Porte d'Italie, Paris, are complemented by candlesticks from Nuit Blanche.

The dining room is dominated by a Hubert Le Gall chandelier, surrounded by tall slim cupboards designed by Marchal and a patterned carpet from her boutique Nuit Blanche.

In the entrance hall Marchal has used a wealth of trompe l'oeil paint and molding effects. In the center is a Biedermeier table bought at auction by the decorator.

The painted wallpaper from Colefax and Fowler provide a rich background for the thick-striped contemporary covering of the sofas. The curtains are in white linen, while the flowery embroidered carpet was especially ordered from India.

OPPOSITE THE PICASSO MUSEUM, in one of the oldest historic areas of Paris, is the Galerie Frédéric Mechiche. It provides a dazzling showcase for the talent of one of Paris's leading interior designers, who also creates some of his own furniture. Versatile and innovative, he is equally comfortable designing a small apartment or a Renaissance château, and has fulfilled numerous commissions for both. He has one golden rule: "First create the perfect base, then plan the decoration; mood and atmosphere can be introduced in many different ways, but the base remains unchanged." He continues, "You have to ask yourself what sort of atmosphere you want to create; how you would entertain different numbers of people; where to put the television, the music center, and the telephone; where you want to sit and read and so on. The distribution of each individual element needs to be worked out well in advance, otherwise it will destroy the atmosphere." Mechiche has a strong eye for proportion and detail, as well as a love for the authentic and genuine, but does not overlook imaginative personal touches. As he says, "I like mixing old elements with new and putting good-quality pieces with funny little souvenirs. It gives a room personality and charm."

A picture collection is arranged above Mechiche's postmodern furniture, which is given a sharp relief by the strong purple of the tablecloth and the violet-cushioned, wrought-iron chairs.

The bathroom features a spectacular free-standing bath, whose curves dictate the alcoved paneling and their pastoral painted scenes. Mechiche's talent is to use period elements to create an unmistakably twentieth-century atmosphere.

The designer's Paris apartment is a white backdrop to his book collection and his beautifully sensual furniture. Some are covered in an original zebra skin style textile, repeated in the rug on the polished Parisian parquet floor.

In this light and airy salon corner, a timeless Mechiche sofa and chair in a
pale striped fabric have a cool refined elegance typical of the designer. Here
it is set against peach silk curtains and a traditional parquet floor.

Chahan
MINASSIAN

CHAHAN MINASSIAN BEGAN HIS PROFESSIONAL career as European creative director for Polo Ralph Lauren, where he was responsible for the stores' development and interior design in over ten European countries. In 1993 he set up his own company, Chahan, and he has quickly become one of the leading lights of the younger generation of Parisian designers, creating Patrick Cox's stores across the world and numerous international commissions for private apartments. His own apartment, in constant evolution, shows Minassian's eclectic eye and delight in creating a personal atmosphere. He emphasizes a rich range of texture and the eschewing of aggressive colors, creating an atmosphere of soothing tonality. Chahan Minassian says of his decoration, "I never try to reconstruct a precise period. I allow myself to be guided by the diversity of textures and materials and by the stories that furniture and objects tell."

A coffee table sits behind an American sofa of the 1940s that is covered with precious silks and a tiger skin. The mantelpiece behind is dominated by the head of an ephebe, which came from a garden in Newport. Wall fittings that flank the mirror are by André Dubreuil.

Minassian's salon is bathed in a golden light from an Arte Luce candelabra, originally designed for a theater in the 1950s. In the foreground is an immense golden sphere designed by Minassian himself. On either side of the 1930s ivory laquered table are two lamps by Samuel Marx that are supported by parchment-covered columns; a voluptuous fur rug lies on the parquet floor.

The geometrical purity of the dining room serves as a good background to the American 1950s lamps and the 1930s table. The chairs are signed Robsjohn-Gibbing, an American designer of the 1950s.

Chahan Minassian's bed, covered by a Ralph Lauren plaid, is dominated by a curious 1940s wrought iron headboard, above which hangs the designer's personal collection of pictures and drawings.

PATRICK ELIE NAGGAR IS A FRENCH ARTIST, architect, and designer born in Egypt. He received his degree in architecture from the École des Beaux Arts and a masters degree in urban studies from the University of Paris. Naggar considers architecture to be a central knowledge, encompassing interior design and furniture design; a catalyst for ideas, forms, plastic, and artistic trends in order to create objects and spaces for our environment in the spirit of our times. Naggar divides his time between Paris and New York, bringing his painterly eye (Naggar frequently exhibits as a painter) for combining myth, the modern, and the industrial in interior designs both in Europe and the United States, where with his partner, Terese Carpenter, he has founded Nile, Inc. He also works extensively for an elite private clientele, as well as numerous commercial design projects, including the perfume line of Paloma Picasso and offices for Yves Saint Laurent in New York. His furniture was the subject of a one-man show in New York at the Gallery of the Applied Arts in October 1985, and at Arc International in 1991.

Naggar's chairs and table make a stylish, contemporary dining area.

In the bedroom, the designer uses rich, wooden built-in cabinets to provide essential warmth amid the contemporary idiom. The cabinets are set at a low level to compensate for the relatively low ceiling,

In this Swiss chalet, Naggar designed all the furniture and fittings for the clients. In the salon, lit by dormer windows, *canapés* and chairs gather around a custom-built chimney in a pale cream and blue color scheme.

For these clients, who collect twentieth-century artwork, Naggar designed a special display area for a watering can by Raynaud.

Naggar's design for this chair is based on an eighteenth-century design of an astronomer's star-gazing chair.

A sleek, peach pedestal supports the streamlined bathroom basin.

THE DECORATION PARTNERSHIP of Sylvie Nègre and Violaine d'Harambure, whose headquarters are in the refined 16th arrondissement of Paris, has been in operation for the past twenty-five years. They apply their wealth of experience to projects ranging from the simple renovation of an apartment to large-scale commissions such as the bijou luxury hotel Montaigne on Paris's leading fashion avenue of the same name. Nègre particularly likes late eighteenth- and early nineteenth-century decoration and furniture. She has a sober approach to an essentially cosseting style of interior design, but also enjoys conceiving ingenious staircases and mezzanines, reflecting her passionate interest in all things that contribute to pure architectural lines. The partnership is based on a rapport in which both decorators share and participate equally in the finished project. In addition to a discerning private clientele, they have also been invited to create installations at the important Biennale des Antiquaires in Paris, producing their own brand of distinctive Right Bank chic.

A classically French salon in Sylvie Nègre's Paris apartment. Alongside the Louis XV furniture, there are discreet modern touches, such as the reading lamps and wicker coffee table, as well as a collection of contemporary art.

Another view of the salon reveals the full double height of the room with its classical moldings and mirrors.

Nègre's directoire-style mezzanine was designed to make maximum use of the high ceilings without destroying the proportions of the original apartment.

Nègre uses the mezzanine as an office area. The room benefits from a classical striped wallpaper.

A sweeping staircase leads into the entrance hall, which is dominated by a huge twentieth-century Venetian chandelier. On the opposite wall Nègre echoes the original staircase, making this space very much the center of the apartment.

PATRICE NOURISSAT GRADUATED from the celebrated Camondo School of Interior Architecture and Design, Paris. He spent six years of apprenticeship with one of the great figures of Parisian interior design, Didier Aaron. In 1977 he opened his own practice and enjoys the patronage of an exclusive national and inter-national clientele. Nourissat favors close personal relationships with his clients and respects their privacy and taste. Recent commissions have included large private homes in Istanbul, Warsaw, Barcelona, Vienna, and Geneva, as well as important Parisian projects, including the spectacular renovation of a nineteenth-century artist's studio. Nourissat's interiors are immediately recognizable by a certain liberty and sense of fantasy that he brings to his work while always retaining a professional rigor in their execution. Even his own offices reject the mundane Right or Left Bank designer streets in favor of Paris's up and coming 20th arrondissement, very much in keeping with this out of the ordinary Parisian designer.

One of the designer's carved wooden panels features a medley of kitchen implements, emphasizing the grand country atmosphere.

The designer's spectacular salon with a jungle of green plants is kept healthy by a humidification system. The chimney piece shows Nourissat at his most flamboyant, where the ensemble is an exciting mix of a rough terra-cotta tiled floor and exposed stone walls with a highly sophisticated collection of sculpture and decorative elements.

A pure vermilion wall is a chance to appreciate Nourissat's strong theatricality.
The wall dramatically encloses a pale stone fireplace, decorated by black and
silver vases, creating a tonal yet visually arresting effect.

High-backed dining chairs and a collection of pewter give the grand baronial
dining room a Renaissance atmosphere.

FROM HIS STYLISHLY GRAND OFFICES on the banks of the river Seine, Alberto Pinto directs one of Paris's most successful interior design companies. His name is a byword for elegant Parisian decoration, but Pinto began his career in charge of a photographic agency that specialized in images of architecture and decoration. While on shoots in Italy, Pinto was able to develop his taste for design. In Mexico, with Luis Baragan, he discovered a use of space and color, and in England was able to admire the *savoir faire* of David Hicks. All these diverse experiences resulted in the opening of his own studio in the 1970s, and since that time he has been responsible for some of the most prestigious projects in France, as well as more intimate private projects. Pinto has the talent to understand and respect the eclectic tastes of his French and international clients, and remains a master in the art of creating made-to-measure homes in which the elegance is reflected by a balanced sense of abundance.

A cleverly back-lit glass panel creates a Jules Verne–like aquarium sensation.

Pinto's designs for an ocean liner hark back to a more opulent age. The rich sea-blue fabrics and carpet underline the maritime message, as do the designer's frescoed pillars.

An ingenious dressing room uses old-fashioned wicker hampers instead of drawers, and includes a club-style black leather chair.

A typical Pinto composition in black and gold, this Chinese coromandel screen is surrounded by hand-painted wooden classical columns.

An elegant bathroom decorated with a blue Wedgewood medallion and jug, where the button-backed chair adds a British touch to the room.

The patterned carpet spills over from the bathroom into the master bedroom. Furniture and objects are Napoleon III, and a writing area is neatly separated by a folding screen.

ELEGANCE AND COMFORT are the priorities of decorator Lillan Pons-Seguin, and for the past fifteen years these joint concerns have brought her commissions from across Europe for hotels, private houses, and apartments. Practical and feminine, she has a perfectionist's eye for detail and does not hesitate to design her own carpets, sofas, and fabrics if the unity of the project calls for it. She is equally at home with the dyeing and restoration of antique fabrics, collaborating with a network of experienced artisans. In order to give each project her full attention, she voluntarily limits her activities to one or two large commissions per year. The rest of the time she spends between Paris and her country home, where she annually designs two or three collections of her own household linen, which she sells at her boutique Nouez-moi in the chic 16th arrondissement. It is an ideal address at which to buy a present from amongst the embroidered and monogrammed household linens or accessories, all with that elegant Pons-Seguin touch.

Floral fabric and deep sofas give the room an English cottage feel, an effect emphasized by the jumble of books and magazines on the coffee table and the bookcase and writing desk behind.

The kitchen is dominated by a collection of blue and white porcelain, which is the key to the decoration of the whole room. The open fire gives way to a rustic refectory table flanked by kitchen chairs with blue and white cushions matching the fabric of the curtains of the designer's cupboards.

An overview of a Pons-Seguin salon reveals a daring color scheme of straw yellow and vermilion. The room is home to a collection of contemporary art, but nonetheless exudes a very feminine sense of comfort and well-being, with the matching side tables, lamps, tablecloths, and well-cushioned sofas.

The long nineteenth-century hall table holds a collection of blue and white Chinese vases and urns. The matching pair of green shaded lamps shows the influence of Madeleine Castaing.

With its tented garland-motif fabric against lime green walls, the dining room has a more contemporary atmosphere. Cushioned wrought iron chairs keep company with the nineteenth-century French wrought iron chandelier.

Andrée
PUTMAN

A FÊTED PARISIAN CELEBRITY, Andrée Putman is recognized as something of an archaeologist of modernity. In 1978 Putman founded a company with the objective of rediscovering forgotten figures of early twentieth-century design who are now acknowledged masters such as Eileen Gray, Jean Michel Frank, Pierre Chareau, Robert Mallet Stevens, and Mariano Fortuny. With the zeal of a scientist she reproduced their furniture and objects from the original drawings. She also began to discover new young talents to whom she brought her formidable commercial expertise. Putman seeks to redefine the function of a decorator, an appellation she rejects with vehemence. She prefers to adapt volume and light, rather than saturate the space with decorative details. Her refined spatial harmony and use of neutral colors give Putman's work a timeless fashion-resistant quality. Her private clients remain just that, but amongst her many business designs are commissions from major fashion figures such as Lagerfeld, Mugler, and Yves Saint Laurent. As well as for hotels, such as Morgans in New York, Putman designs for the cinema and exhibitions, notably Peter Greenaway's *Pillow Book* and the *Rendez-vous: Pompidou Guggenheim* exhibition in New York.

White frosted glass separates the dining area from the kitchen. The minimalist approach directs attention to Putman's stylish twentieth-century chairs and the curving lines of the spiral staircase.

In a Parisian artist's studio, a dining area mingles with the traditional easel work space. Notice the elegant glass and chrome balustrade of the mezzanine.

Putman's twentieth-century four-poster bed has a striking formal purity. The rich wood is echoed in the paneling into which dramatic low level lights are incorporated.

MORE THAN A TOUCH OF FEMININE SENSUALITY runs through the work and personality of Dominique Racine. She began her career in 1987, establishing a fine reputation with a private clientele who appreciate her taste for authentic French *savoir vivre.* "To know how to draw" is the talent Racine sees as quintessential to the work of a designer. She is herself a fine draftswoman and spends days at the drawing board, imagining the daily lives of her clients, their needs and requirements, envisioning everything, including the vital importance of natural light on the finished design. Her own taste is for the genuine comfort of bygone times; yet Racine is a polished professional, aware of the need for practical storage and all the realities of contemporary life. She defines her style as "the conveying of a lifestyle, never flashy, and always mindful of charm and comfort. I do not like the falsely clinical, the perfectly straight, the impeccable. It's a lie. I couldn't possibly read *Le Vicomte de Bragelonne* in a high tech loft."

A Louis XVI bureau provides an informal working area in a bedroom corner.

Red *toile de Jouy* wall covering adds a luxurious touch to the bedroom. It also lines the red-striped curtains, which are draped to reveal a further striped blind. The overall effect is one of cosseting comfort, with a book-laden Bamboo table for late night reading.

The salon is dominated by the *haute époque* chimney and *chaufferette* chair. As Racine particularly dislikes the sofa–coffee table combination, attractive tapestry stools serve as tables. A rustic Provençale sofa contrasts with a striking leopard-skin sofa.

Racine favors blue and white in her kitchen designs, demonstrated here by a collection of blue porcelain hung on the rear wall. The wooden church-style benches and waxed rustic table create a warm country atmosphere, emphasized by the lamps converted from ancient storage jars.

A simple frieze of Racine's favorite blue tiling adorns the alcoved preparation area, together with some more attractive porcelain.

"THE GILBERT AND GEORGE OF DESIGN" was how *Vogue* magazine recently described the work of Clements **RA**meckers and Arnold **VA**n **GE**uns, who combined their names to form the design partnership Ravage. Born in the same month of the same year, these two creative artists studied together at the Beaux Arts Academy of Arnhem in their native Netherlands. Their personal and professional collaboration flourished, establishing their own gallery in Paris in 1976, where their very personal reinterpretation of design and history caught the eye of Karl Lagerfeld amongst many others. Their zany off-the-wall style often reflects the duality of their own relationship: pictures, china, collage and furniture designed around Adam and Eve, hope and joy, or even EDF and GDF (the French electricity and gas companies). The mixture of fake and anecdotal original makes for work that mocks the prosaic but nonetheless is designed with professional rigor in collaboration with leading manufacturers. Their country home in France shows a restrained Ravage idyll. As they say, "We are not furniture designers but atmosphere makers."

A view of the dining room with French windows opening onto the Normandy countryside. The lacy antimacassars are a typical tongue-in-cheek Ravage touch.

Ravage went for dacha-style for their rich blue dining room. A profusion of their own custom-made porcelain, both on the walls and on the table, completes the room.

The salon features a typical Ravage double wall-hanging with porcelain panels, matched by a pair of side lamps and another pair of miniature pictures. The chairs are draped in white sheets around a coffee table covered in a Ravage fabric and a comforting collection of objects.

The bedroom is dominated by Ravage's own pictures, which hang around a simple country-style four-poster wooden bed. The whole room has a light and airy color scheme, the ideal backdrop for the artwork.

The bathroom area of the bedroom is dominated by Ravage ceramics in cream and black; old-fashioned fittings repeat the country style of the whole house.

ONE OF FRANCE'S BRIGHTEST young designers, Jean-Louis Riccardi was first apprenticed to Jacques Grange, then spent four years with Madeleine Castaing, where, as he says, "The timeless world of poetry and atmosphere became apparent to me." Setting up on his own, he has quickly gained an international clientele, including the fashion giant Christian Lacroix, actress Fanny Ardant, and one of the grandest hotels in Paris, the Hotel de Crillon. Riccardi is also one of the favored designers for leading antique and fashion galleries, where his passion for people is fully explored. "What I love above all else in my work is meeting with my clients and their dreams. To listen and exchange ideas, the surprises, the fantasy, the intimacy . . . all these shared emotions that will make their dream a reality."

An ethnic sculpture on a stone plinth in front of a wrought iron screen are part of a beige and cream collection that gives this corner a chic contemporary look.

A second Empire gothic revival bureau is home to a profusion of iconographic images, including a picture on the wall by Jean Jacques Henner. The richness of the fabrics and the picture hangings create a strong Proustian atmosphere.

In this elaborately draped salon, the influence of Madeleine Castaing can be felt more strongly, but Riccardi brings a very personal lavishness to his designs.

Some fabric samplers and a dress-maker's dummy are the theme of this Marie Antoinette–style room. The commode is Louis XVI, and the whole room is painted in a light-washed polichrome of the subtlest tones.

The only touch of color in an entirely curtained *fin de siècle* room is from twentieth-century glass candles on both tables.

A second Empire vase sets the tone for this extravagant bathroom. The walls are draped, and the bath itself surrounded in a gold leaf casing.

Eric SCHMITT

ERIC SCHMITT BEGAN HIS CAREER in a saddle as a show jumper and was a member of the French team for five years. After a brief flirtation with contemporary music, he found his true voice in the 1980s, forging his own furniture and objects. In 1987 he held his first exhibition, where his creations in bronze, wrought iron, and ceramics caught the imagination of critics and public alike. "Suddenly I felt involved. I understood that a certain volume could make a piece of furniture interesting, and not the ornamentation, which is there as a finish. I had become a real furniture maker." Schmitt's work frequently evokes his admiration and special respect for Tinguely and Alberto Giacometti. But in terms of mastery of volume and symmetry, it is the classical grandeur of the architect Nicolas Ledoux to whom he turns for inspiration. In 1990 Christian Liaigre ordered work from him for the Montalembert Hotel and a year later his collection was exhibited by the Galerie Néotù in Paris and New York. This rigorously anti-intellectual creative artisan enjoys Cocteau's definition of fashion as "that which becomes unfashionable."

In the bedroom, a wooden plinth bed and fine-legged bedside table rely on the architectural purity and warmth of the natural wood for their effect.

Schmitt designed all of the furniture and fittings in this salon, which is home to the client's collection of photography. The grey and brown hues of the canapés join in with the play of different woods in the side tables and coffee table.

Seen from the drawing room, Schmitt's finely wrought furniture and neutral colors create an uncluttered space that highlights the room's fine proportions.

In Schmitt's own kitchen, functional, elegant furniture mingles with discreet, contemporary black and white cupboards. A wrought iron tripod stands beside a red lacquered door that provides a burst of color.

An original console with circular wooden motifs set against a white background shows the designer at his functional and decorative best.

Yves
TARALON

FOR MORE THAN THIRTY YEARS, the decorator Yves Taralon has been dedicated to the observation of what makes up *le gout français*. Born in the heart of France, he has retained from his country upbringing a certain calm serenity, an appreciation of the work of artisans, a respect for the quality of materials, and a love of gastronomy and the French way of life. After designing numerous apartments for prominent figures of the press and the fashion world, he began to work for an impressive list of top companies, including Baccarat, Lacoste, Actuel, Hédiard, Guerlain, Rochas, Rémy Martin, and Bally. He became known to the general public through the creation of fashionable meeting places in the grand literary café tradition: in Paris, the Café Marly under the arches of the Louvre, the tearoom of the Musée Jacquemard-André, and the Café Niki in Tokyo. Currently he is working on the design of a home department for Paris's celebrated Galeries Lafayette. His future plans include a theater in Rio de Janeiro and the restoration of a château in his native Loire valley.

A seemingly casual display of objects, lamps, and books put the focus firmly on the eighteenth-century classical mantelpiece.

The huge wooden logs on either side of the period stone fireplace and the parquet floor are the only elements of the decoration not painted white, making the hearth very much the center of attention.

The dormer window allows light to flood this black and white bathroom. The nineteenth-century bathtub sits on a white stained floor, surrounded by monochromatic art work and a black wrought iron bench.

An archeological vase side view of the salon. The black panther hanging on the back wall sets a mood of tropical colonialism. The 1930s and 1940s modernist furniture sits on a spectacular multicolored rug.

The kitchen is also dominated by a seventeenth-century style bread oven. Wicker garden furniture and white painted beams complete the rustic idyll. The color of the flickering flames is echoed by the sunflowers casually placed at the window.

AS A YOUNGSTER, Pierre Hervé Walbaum took an early interest in antiques and decoration, influenced by his grandfather, who was himself a collector. It was the beginning of a passion that would dominate his life. Against the will of his family, he enrolled at the École des Beaux Arts, where after seven years of study, he obtained a first-class degree in interior architecture.

He spent a further seven years with the Galerie Maison et Jardin, working beside a decorator who was to become his spiritual father, Jean Dives, but for the past twenty years Walbaum has directed his own decoration firm in Paris. He has not lost the bug for collecting and is constantly researching his favorite nineteenth-century neoclassical period. A good number of his clients are also collectors. Walbaum creates and adapts spaces for them to display their works of art and pictures to best advantage. Most of his projects are in France but he also works in the United States and Great Britain. He says of his work, "The most important element is the personality of the client. You have to analyze their way of life in order to create a link between place and client, at the same time investing the project with soul."

The library converts into an intimate dining room. The green turtle shell "cartel" is Louis XV, a color picked up in the especially made wallpaper. The center light is of the Restoration period, subtly capturing the eighteenth-century embroidered tablecloth and Saxe dinner service.

An eighteenth-century terra-cotta statue dominates this entrance hall, lit by a lantern of the same period. Red silk curtains and an ornamental eighteenth-century column complete the formal arrangement.

You can appreciate an impressive picture by Gaspar du Guet, opposite an originally designed bookcase which functions as a library. The chairs were made by the eighteenth-century ebonist Fourdinois for the Empress Eugénie's yacht, *l'Hirondelle.*

A view of the salon shows the seventy-light chandelier and the Louis XVI sofa, as well as the authentic silk velvet covering for the tables.

JEAN-MICHEL WILMOTTE IS A GRADUATE of the celebrated Camondo School and formed his own company in 1975. He now employs a team of seventy people of different nationalities: architects, town planners, interior architects, and designers, with whom he works on major national and international projects for private and business clients. To begin with, Wilmotte concentrated on designing contemporary furniture and interior architecture, notably in the world of museums, where his work can be appreciated in the Richelieu wing of the restored Louvre. Now, from giving a contemporary look to ancient buildings, his work has extended to full-fledged architecture, and recently a department of industrial design has been established. In the last few years he has, in addition, developed the concept of "interior architecture for towns," a new approach to the treatment of urban spaces that deals with recladding (floors, walls, and façades), park areas, lighting, urban design and transport; in this area his work has included an airport terminal at Paris CDG and a project to give the Champs Elysées some elegant new trimmings. Recently he was responsible for Monaco's pavilion at the EXPO '98 in Lisbon. His interior design work represents contemporary minimalism at its Gallic best.

The architectural structure is outlined in bordeaux in a pure white design with tables repeating the intense blue of the twentieth-century artwork.

In this rehabilitation of an historic building, the restored bare stone walls serve as a backdrop for the simple lines of Wilmotte's contemporary furniture.

The architect skillfully transformed a period space with a mezzanine, separated from the room by an original pierced screen. An industrially inspired sliding door serves as both shutter and curtain.

A beamed bedroom benefits from Wilmotte's strong minimalist furniture, which emphasizes the beauty of the wood and makes the most of the room's proportions.

In a Turkish bath, Wilmotte reworks in massive wood the traditional loungers; the atmosphere nonetheless remains contemporary.

Tino ZERVUDACHI

180

TINO ZERVUDACHI, WHOSE EXOTIC sounding name is explained by a Greek father and an Irish mother, has been working in Paris with the decorator David Milinaric, with whom he trained, for the past eight years. The company has its Paris headquarters in the colonnaded arcade that surrounds the beautiful gardens of the Palais Royal, but they also have offices in London and New York. Zervudachi works for an exclusive private clientele across Europe and in the United States. He is unusually flexible in his approach to decoration, endeavoring to discover exactly what the client has in mind. His decoration is always in accord with the architectural style of the place in question. So, be it a Moroccan-style villa in the South of France or a book-lined apartment for a collector in Virginia, he is happy to respond to the required period or style, often designing the details himself. From the past generation he admires the late Henri Samuel, with whom he shares a total professionalism and a rigorous attention to detail, which typify the best in French decoration.

Despite an Arts and Crafts easy chair, the bathroom has a Moroccan atmosphere lent by the Islamic mosaic and North African lantern; a latticed wooden screen provides a bridge between the two styles.

The British Arts and Crafts style of this home is most noticeable in the library, where the center light, bookcase, and chimney piece are all typical of the period, including the dark green walls topped by an Arts and Crafts frieze.

The bedroom contains a subtle marriage of periods: A softer grey and cream contemporary aspect mingles with the Arts and Crafts style sofa and side cupboard.

The dining room features a set of Arts and Crafts dining chairs with their typical high backs. The color scheme is an unusual contrast of saffron and powder blue above the cornice, where a collection of porcelain of the same period hangs.

Photo CREDITS

Cover photo by Brian Harrison, design by Thierry Virvaire.

Photos on pages 4–5, from left to right, also appear respectively on pages 66–67, 96, 100, 117, 136–137, 146, 164.

Photos on pages 6–7, from left to right, also appear respectively on pages 21, 41, 61, 96, 113, 166.

Photos on pages 8–9, from left to right, also appear respectively on pages 26, 65, 77, 87, 90, 149, 154.

Photography for Christian Badin (pages 10–15)
by Guillaume de Laubier

Photography for Claudio Briganti (pages 16–19)
by Ali Von Bothmer

Photography for Manuel Canovas (pages 20–23)
by Guillaume de Laubier

Photography for Madeleine Castaing (pages 24–29)
by Roland Beaufre (pages 24, 26, 28 and 29)
and Guillaume de Laubier (pages 24 bottom, 25, and 27)

Photography for François Catroux (pages 30–35)
by Marianne Haas

Photography for Eric Caspers Ciborowski (pages 36–41)
by Roland Beaufre

Photography for Agnes Comar (pages 42–45)
by Guillaume de Laubier

Photography for Robert d'Ario (pages 46–51)
by Arthur Peguin (pages 46, 48 and 50)
and Antoine Schramm (pages 47, 49 and 51)

Photography for Alain Demachy (pages 52–55)
by Marianne Haas (pages 52 and 53) and
Alain Demachy (pages 54 and 55)

Photography for Olivier Gagnère (pages 56–59)
by Guillaume de Laubier

Photography for Laurent Galle (pages 60–63)
by Wilfrid Rouff

Photography for Jacques Garcia (pages 64–69)
by Guillaume de Laubier

Photography for Henri Garelli (pages 70–73)
by Roland Beaufre

Photography for Garouste and Bonetti (pages 74–77)
by Guillaume de Laubier

Photography for Eric Gizard (pages 78–81)
by Roland Beaufre

Photography for Didier Gomez (pages 82–85)
by Guillaume de Laubier

Photography for François-Joseph Graf (pages 86–89)
by Guillaume de Laubier

Photography for Jacques Grange (pages 90–95)
by Roland Beaufre

Photography for Michelle Halard (pages 96–99)
by Guillaume de Laubier

Photography for Daniel Hamel (pages 100–103)
by Olivier Ferrer

Photography for Jacques Leguennec (pages 104–107)
by Guillaume de Laubier

Photography for Christian Liaigre (pages 108–113)
by Jacques Dirand

Photography for Sabine Marchal (pages 114–117)
by Vincent Knapp

Photography for Frédéric Mechiche (pages 118–121)
by Jacques Dirand (pages 118 and 119)
and Guillaume de Laubier (pages 120 and 121)

Photography for Chahan Minassian (pages 122–125)
by Sylvain Thomas

Photography for Patrick Elie Naggar (pages 126–129)
by Christophe Kicherer

Photography for Sylvie Nègre (pages 130–133)
by Chevallier

Photography for Patrice Nourissat (pages 134–137)
by Jacques Dirand

Photography for Alberto Pinto (pages 138–143)
by Roland Beaufre

Photography for Lillan Pons-Seguin (pages 144–147)
by Jacques Dirand

Photography for Andrée Putman (pages 148–151)
by Deidi Von Schaewen

Photography for Dominique Racine (pages 152–155)
by Guillaume de Laubier

Photography for Ravage (pages 156–159)
by Van Den Berg

Photography for Jean-Louis Riccardi (pages 160–163)
by Roland Beaufre

Photography for Eric Schmitt (pages 164–167)
by J. P. Godeaut

Photography for Yves Taralon (pages 168–171)
by Roland Beaufre

Photography for Pierre Hervé Walbaum (pages 172–175)
by Roland Beaufre

Photography for Jean-Michel Wilmotte (pages 176–179)
by Robert Cesar

Photography for Tino Zervudachi (pages 180–183)
by Roland Beaufre

Christian Badin
52 rue Bourgogne
Paris 75007

Claudio Briganti
4 rue des Abbesses
Paris 75018

Manuel Canovas
7 rue Furstenberg
Paris 75006

Madeleine Castaing
21 rue Bonaparte
Paris 75006

François Catroux
20 rue du Faubourg Saint Honoré
Paris 75008

Eric Caspers Ciborowski
85 bis, rue Billancourt
Boulogne 92000

Agnes Comar
7 avenue George V
Paris 75008

Robert d'Ario
9 rue des Coffres
Toulouse 31000

Alain Demachy
Galerie Camoin
9 quai Voltaire
Paris 75007

Olivier Gagnère
47 Boulevard St. Jacques
Paris 75014

Laurent Galle
23 rue Chevert
Paris 75007

Jacques Garcia
212 rue Rivoli
Paris 75001

Henri Garelli
75 Rue Notre Dame des Champs
Paris 75006

Garouste and Bonetti
14 rue Moulin Joly
Paris 75011

Eric Gizard
6 rue Jules Chaplain
Paris 75006

Didier Gomez
Ory Gomez
15 rue Henri Heine
Paris 75016

François-Joseph Graf
Ariodante
17 rue de Lille
Paris 75007

Jacques Grange
118 rue du Faubourg Saint Honoré
Paris 75008

Michelle Halard
Yves Halard
252 bis Boulevard Saint Germain
Paris 75007

Daniel Hamel
61 rue du Faubourg Saint Honoré
Paris 75008

Jacques Leguennec
J. L. Diffusion
9 rue Casimir Delavigne
Paris 75006

Christian Liaigre
61 rue de Varenne
Paris 75007

Sabine Marchal
41 rue de Bourgogne
Paris 75007

Frédéric Mechiche
4 rue Thorigny
Paris 75003

Chahan Minassian
3 rue de la Planche
Paris 75007

Patrick Elie Naggar
189 rue St. Honoré
Paris 75001

Sylvie Nègre
Violaine D'Harambure
37 rue Raynouard
Paris 75016

Patrice Nourissat
230 rue des Pyrénées
Paris 75020

Alberto Pinto
61 quai d'Orsay
Paris 75007

Lillan Pons-Seguin
Nouez-moi
27 rue des Sablons
Paris 75016

Andrée Putman
83 avenue Denfert Rochereau
Paris 75014

Dominique Racine
6 rue Gaston de Paul
Paris 75016

Ravage
Cours des Fabriques
70 rue Jean-Pierre Timbaud
Paris 75011

Jean-Louis Riccardi
30 rue Vineuse
Paris 75016

Eric Schmitt
10 rue de Nemours
Villiers sous Grez 77760

Yves Taralon
47 bis rue Bretagne
Paris 75003

Pierre Hervé Walbaum
12 rue Alger
Paris 75001

Jean-Michel Wilmotte
68 rue du Faubourg Saint-Antoine
Paris 75012

Tino Zervudachi
Milinaric, Henry and Zervudachi
54, Galerie de Montpensier
Jardin du Palais Royal
Paris 75001

About the
AUTHOR

BORN IN DEVON, ENGLAND, Stephen Mudge has been, since an early age, passionately interested in all things French. His profession as a musician led him to live in his favorite city, Paris, where he began writing about his experiences in the capital. This activity led to a whole new career, contributing articles to *Woman and Home* on everything from food to furniture. He is a food critic for *Time Out* in Paris, correspondent for *Opera News,* and also writes for the BBC *Food and Drink* magazine. He is currently finishing his first novel and researching a book on Parisian museums.

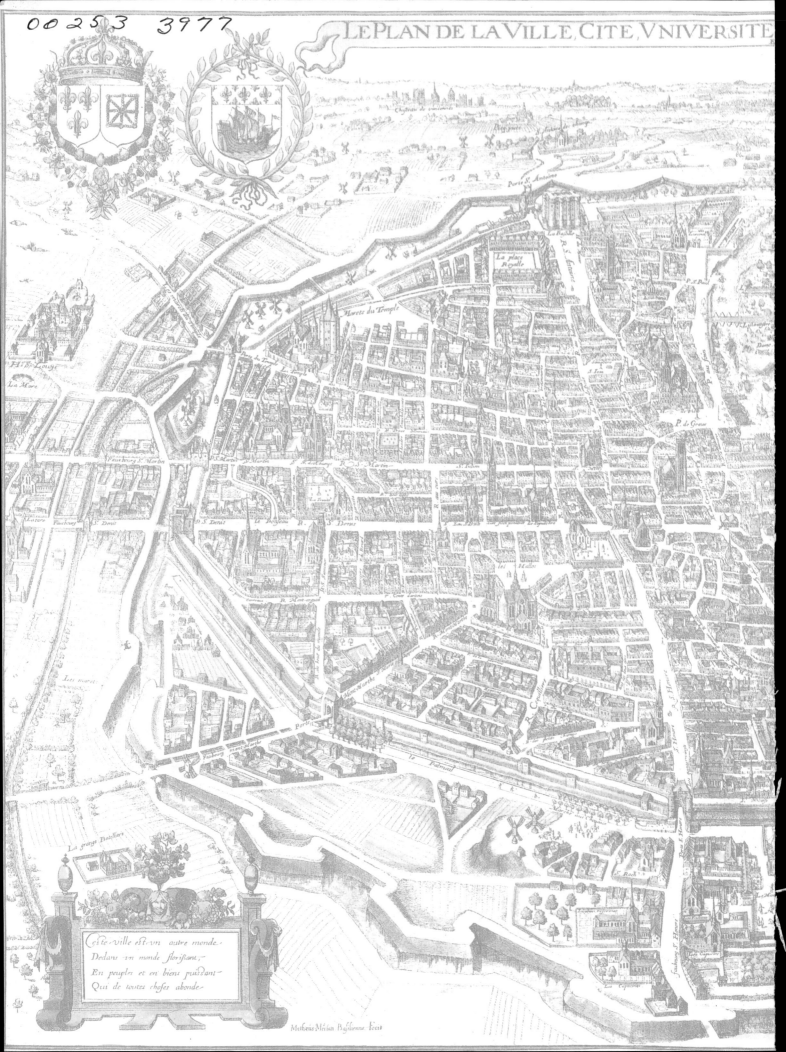

LE PLAN DE LA VILLE, CITE, VNIVERSITE

Cette ville est vn autre monde
Dedans vn monde florissant,
En peuples et en biens puissant
Qui de toutes choses abonde